Creating BOTTLES with GOURDS & FIBER

Jim Widess

Title Page image: Hue wai pawehe — Decorated Hawaiian water gourd.
Courtesy of David Young, artist.

Other Schiffer Books on Related Subjects:
Weaving on Gourds, 978-0-7643-3565-5, $19.99
Historic Gourd Craft: How to Make Traditional Vessels,
978-0-7643-2830-5, $14.95
Coiled Designs for Gourd Art, 978-0-7643-3011-7, $14.99
Antler Art for Baskets and Gourds, 978-0-7643-3615-7, $19.99

Copyright © 2011 by Jim Widess
Unless otherwise noted, all images are the property of the author.
Library of Congress Control Number: 2011934274

Designed by Justin Watkinson Cover by Bruce Waters
Type set in Humanst521 BT/New Baskerville

ISBN: 978-0-7643-3866-3
Printed in China

Schiffer Books are available at special discounts for bulk pur-
chases for sales promotions or premiums. Special editions, in-
cluding personalized covers, corporate imprints, and excerpts
can be created in large quantities for special needs. For more
information contact the publisher:

Published by Schiffer Publishing Ltd.
4880 Lower Valley Road
Atglen, PA 19310
Phone: (610) 593-1777; Fax: (610) 593-2002
E-mail: Info@schifferbooks.com

For the largest selection of fine reference books on this and related
subjects, please visit our website at: **www.schifferbooks.com**
We are always looking for people to write books on new and
related subjects. If you have an idea for a book, please contact
us at **proposals@schifferbooks.com**.

This book may be purchased from the publisher.
Include $5.00 for shipping.
Please try your bookstore first.
You may write for a free catalog.

In Europe, Schiffer books are distributed by
Bushwood Books
6 Marksbury Ave.
Kew Gardens
Surrey TW9 4JF England
Phone: 44 (0) 20 8392 8585; Fax: 44 (0) 20 8392 9876
E-mail: info@bushwoodbooks.co.uk
Website: www.bushwoodbooks.co.uk

ACKNOWLEDGMENTS

We never stop learning. Whether we think we're figuring it out on our own or being guided step-by-step through the process, there are many teachers in the background who exposed us to ways of thinking and analyzing, challenged us by creating intriguing pieces we want to imitate, solved problems with techniques whose solutions now seem lost in our contemporary age.

I want to acknowledge these artisans of the world for creating elegant and beautiful pieces of functionality. In a world without plastic, glass, pottery, and metal, our ancestors discovered that the gourd could move waterfalls and streams so that families could eat and drink in safety. Using strong, flexible fibers from plants and animals, they created structures to make more efficient the comfortable transportation of their precious possessions.

Flo Hoppe deciphered how to weave the foot of the Borneo Cycloid from a couple of photographs sent from Kew Gardens and then taught me. Ginger Summit wove the Malaysian Rinko start, and the Hexagonal Spiral. Marjorie Albright wove the Borneo Cycloid, the Hawaiian Netting, and the Cameroon Palm Wine Bottle.

I am indebted, as always, to my loving and supportive family — my beautiful, artistic wife, Sher, and our wonderfully talented son, Andy — for allowing me these wanderings.

CONTENTS

INTRODUCTION

Gourds have been associated with water and liquids since man first picked up a gourd and had that "ah-ha!" moment of "with this I can bring water to my family to drink in safety." This natural, hard-shelled squash, whose seeds have been found in prehistoric campsites from around the world, was carried out of Africa, through Asia and down the western coast of North America. It's been found on islands throughout the Pacific Ocean. Its use as a vessel for carrying liquids has enshrined it with magical properties, the birth mother of many creation myths and stories, and elaborate reasons why hanging a gourd in one's home will bring good fortune, many children, happiness, prosperity, and long life.

Whether drinking cool, refreshing water on a hot day from a gourd canteen or just taking a quick gulp from the gourd dipper while working in the fields, we are reminded that the gourd has been our water bearer throughout our evolution.

Our family members from Japan, Malaysia, Hawai'i, Borneo, Central America, and Cameroon each used gourds to contain and transport water, rice, or palm wine. I've assembled seven projects showing how each wove a structure around a gourd to make transporting it more accommodating. The projects increase with difficulty as you progress through the seven.

CHAPTER ONE

Japanese Gourd Wine/Water Bottle

WHAT YOU'LL need

ALL Japanese gourd bottles (hyotan) have a wooden stopper that has been drilled to accommodate a satin cord. I have found that few weavers have really studied the knot made with the satin cord that is tied around the waist of the hyotan. The key to the knot is that it is tied with a closed loop. I've also added a tiny gourd for the stopper instead of the traditional wooden one.

- Nicely shaped Mexican or Chinese bottle gourd
- 3 yards of 3.5mm twisted satin cord
- 1 tiny jewelry dipper gourd with long neck and nicely rounded ball or a wooden plug
- Sanding sponges 180, 500, 1000, 5,000, 12,000
- 1/2" drill bit
- 1/4" drill bit
- Electric drill
- Orbital sander
- Awl
- Masking tape
- Needle-nose pliers or crochet hook
- Angelus British Tan leather dye
- Soft cloth for polishing

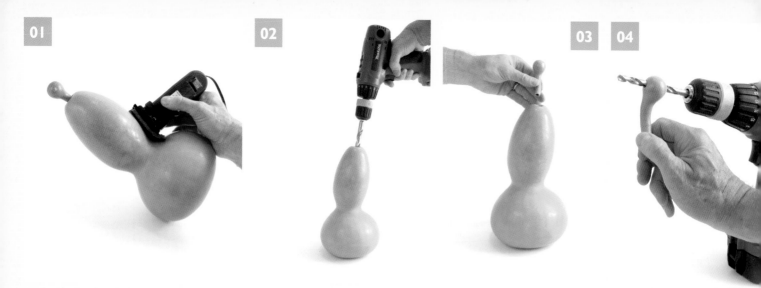

01

Clean gourd shell and wet sand with 180 grit, then 500 grit, 1,000 grit, 5,000 and 12,000 to create a very smooth, glossy surface.

02

Drill a 1/2" hole into the stem end of the gourd. Clean out as much of the guts and seeds as possible. Fill the gourd with water and let it sit for several days. Then pour out the water and guts, add some gravel or nuts and bolts, half fill with water and shake. Spill out the contents and let completely dry.

03

Drop the neck end of your miniature dipper gourd into the opening and fit to make a stopper.

04

Drill a 1/4" hole throug the bulb of the stopper fc the twisted satin cord.

05

Knot #1 is a simple knot similar to an electrician's knot. Make a loop with **A** around **B**, crossing under **B** at **a**, as pictured.

06

Bring **B** over **A** at **b**, under **A** at **c**, then under **A** and **B** a **d**, and over **A** at **e**.

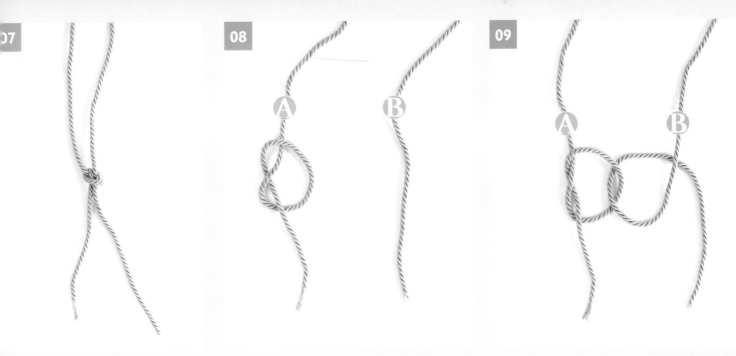

07 Slowly pull the ends of the knot tight and adjust so that it is uniform.

08 Knot #2 is an elegant butterfly knot often found on wine gourds. Make an overhand knot with **A** as pictured above.

09 Bring the end of **B** over, then under, the loop from **A**.

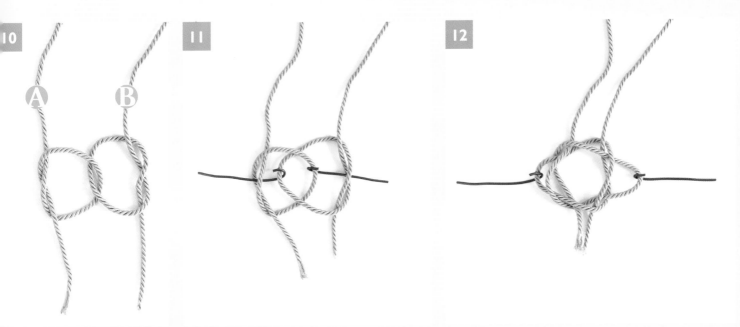

10 Tuck the end of **B** down through the loop you made in the previous step.

11 Separate the two loops in the center and pull them to the outside of the knot (as shown).

12 Continue pulling the loops to the outside through the outside loops.

13

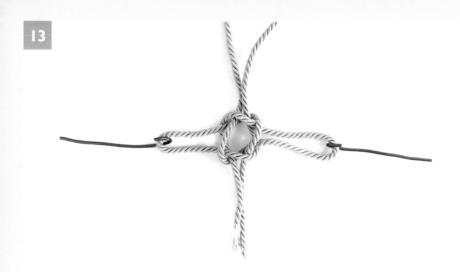

Pull the loops out until the knot is in the proportion that you want it.

14

Tighten up the Butterfly Knot.

15

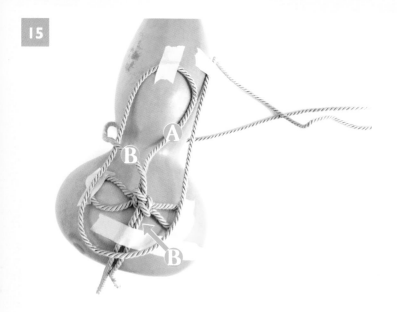

Take the knotted loop of twisted satin cord and use masking tape to tape the knot to the gourd. Bring the left side (**B**) of the loop over **A** and around the back of the gourd.

16

Continue bringing this same part of the loop around the gourd and continue for a 2nd time around

17

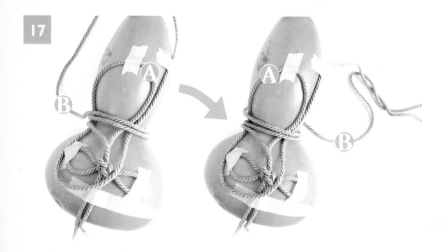

Bring this same loop around for a third time.

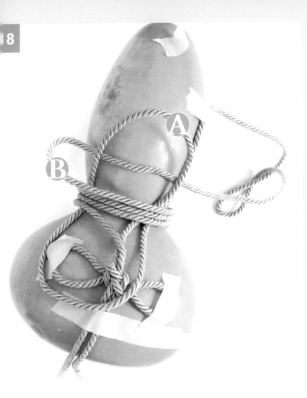

Pull up the slack in the loop you just made around the arc by carefully pulling on the right hand section of the lower loop (c) coming from under the 3 wraps around the waist of the gourd.

...ring the loop around as though you were going ...or a 4th time around, but just make a loop around ...he original arc you made with strand A.

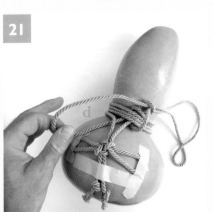

Tighten down the upper loop by carefully pulling on the left hand section of the lower loop (d).

Cinch up the loop so that the entire cord feels snug.

...lip the long, lower loop up through the upper loop ...A) coming from under the 3 wraps at the waist ...f the gourd.

Pass the middle of the long loop through the hole drilled into the gourd stopper. Use needle nose pliers or a crochet hook to pull the loop through the hole.

Pull the end of the loop around the gourd stopper to make a Larks Head knot.

Snug up the Larks Head knot around the stopper. You ca also just pull the loop through and put a knot on the en to keep the stopper from slipping off.

Tie overhand knots 1-2 inches from the ends to keep the cordage from unraveling. Use an awl to separate the individu strands of the end of the twisted satin cord to make a tassel.

This undyed *hyotan* was tied with a maroon satin cord

The completed gourd wine/water bottle: The gourd may be stained or dyed prior to this weaving project. For the photo at the beginning of this chapter, Angelus British Tan leather dye was used.

CHAPTER TWO

Borneo Cycloid

WHAT YOU'LL need

- **Medium to large pear shape gourd**
- **#5.5 (3.50mm) Round Reed**
- **4mm binder cane (rattan peel)**
- **Four 40" lengths of coir (coconut fiber) or other natural fiber for handle**
- **24 twist ties**

THE Cycloid Woven Gourd project is a replica of a gourd canoe bottle we found in the collection of Kew Gardens in London. The gourd was collected in Borneo in 1851. The basketry technique seems to be only practiced by the Dyak tribe of the Iban people of Indonesia. The weaving is simple enough. Each loop locks into the preceding one. In our project we will double the loops for strength. The small hole in the top of the gourd keeps the water from sloshing out of the gourd when carrying it or when the canoe rocks too much. There is a smaller, second hole on the other side of the gourd to allow air to escape or enter the gourd when filling or emptying so that the water flows smoothly.

We will weave two cycloid rings, add a plaited foot to the lower ring, and then lash the two rings together around the body of the gourd. A handle of coconut fiber (coir) completes the project. The footed cycloid woven ring can also be woven as a unique gourd holder without the upper ring and lashing.

WHAT YOU'LL do

- **Choose the longest strand from the coil of #5.5 (3.50mm) round reed.**
- **Soak the strand of round reed in hot tap water for 5 minutes. Do not over-soak. (Note: Over-soaking round reed will make the reed hairy and brittle.)**

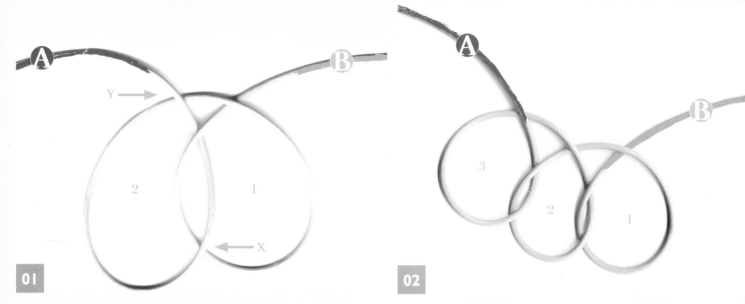

01 Leaving a 12" tail (**B**), make a loop with a strand of round reed and then bring the long end "**A**" over (**X**) and back through loop #1 and then over itself (**Y**) to make loop #2.

02 Pass the end of strand "**A**" over and back through loop #[...] and then over itself. Pull the strand until loop #3 is the sam[...] size as loops #1 and #2.

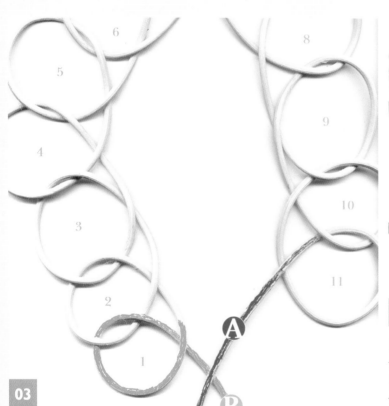

03 Continue making loops until you have eleven full loops. "**B**" (blue) is the short tailpiece from the beginning of the weave.

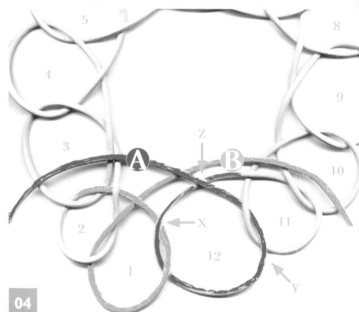

04 Make loop #12 by passing "**A**" (the red strand) over an[...] through the loop #1 (at **X**), then over and through loop #[...] (at **Y**) and then over itself (at **Z**). Carefully study your patter[...] to make sure the insertions are in the correct direction.

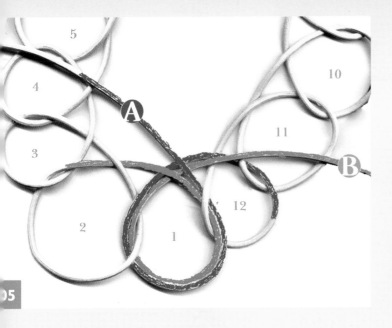

Double the loops: Follow around the outside of loop #1 (in blue) with the long (red) strand "A," doubling the loop. The remainder of (the blue) strand "B" will double inside loop #12. Continue doubling the loops with the long (red) strand "A" until it runs out. Add a new strand and continue until all of the loops are doubled. Leave the ends long, when you add a new strand. We'll cut them in the next step when this ring is completed.

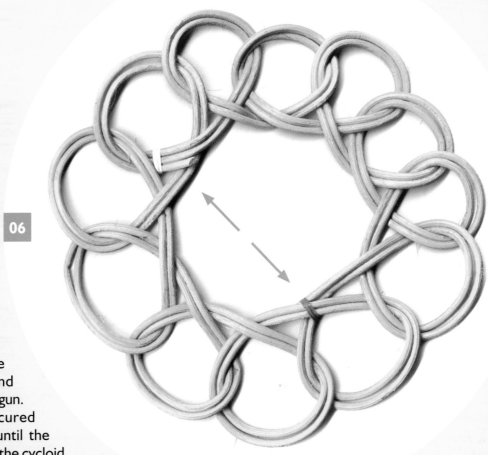

06

Secure the ends of the strands where they are spliced, with a twist tie. The arrows indicate two places where the strand ended and a new strand was begun. These splice points are secured temporarily with twist ties until the moist strands dry. This side of the cycloid disk will be against the gourd, the pressure of which will help anchor the splice points. **Make a 2nd cycloid disk of the same size**.

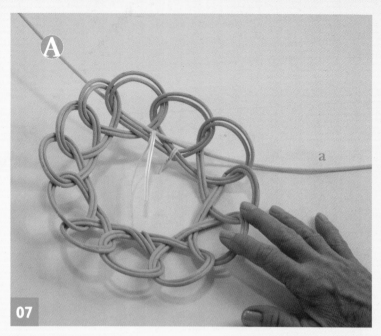

07

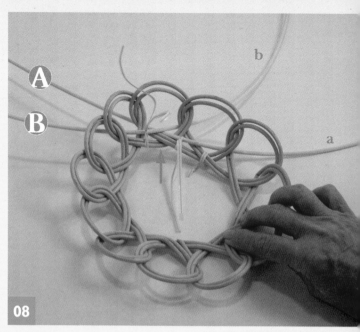

08

Beginning the foot: Cut 12 strands of #5.5 (3.50mm) round reed, 36"long. Weaving the foot will be easier if you label one end of each strand as A, B, C, etc., and you label the other end of each strand as a, b, c, etc. Pass strand Aa up through one loop and out the adjacent loop. Use a twist tie to hold the strand in place. The twist tie should be around the midsection of Aa.

Pass strand Bb up through the adjacent loop to the left, cross over Aa at the arrow, and out the adjacent loop. Secure with twist tie at the midpoint of Bb.

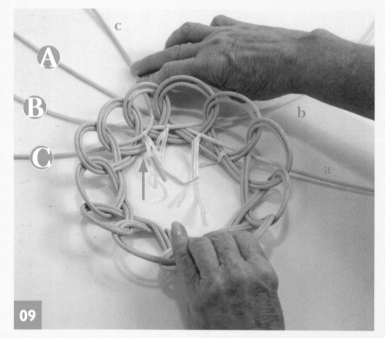

09

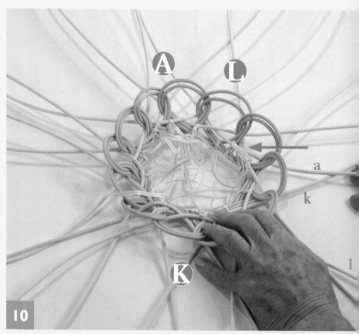

10

Pass strand Cc up through the next loop to the left, cross over Bb at the arrow, and out the adjacent loop. Secure with twist tie at the midpoint of Cc.

Continue adding the foundation strands D-K, in the same fashion, using the twist ties to hold them in position. The final strand Ll will cross over Kk and insert under Aa at the arrow and out the adjacent loop. Secure with a twist tie.

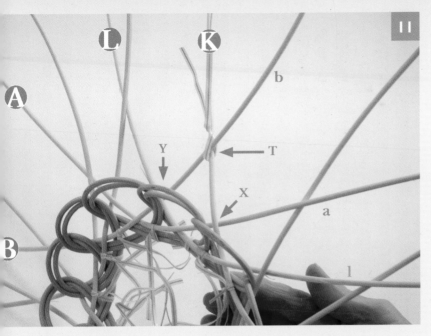

...rand **Kk** will emerge from behind the loop and cross over strand **Aa** ...the arrow "**X**." Strand **Bb** will emerge from behind the loop and ...oss over strand **Ll** at the arrow "**Y**." Use a twist tie to hold **Kk** and ...in position at the arrow "**T**."

Check all of the intersections to make sure that the strands are all weaving over and under and secure the remainder of the crossings.

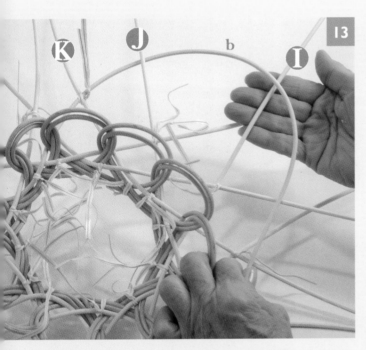

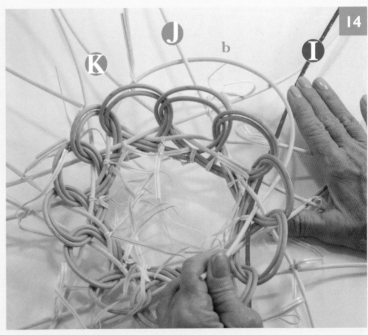

...ck up strand 'b' from its intersection with "K", and pass ...under "J" and then over "I."

Bring strand 'b' along the outer side of "I" (colored red) and under the same strand as "I" at the loop.

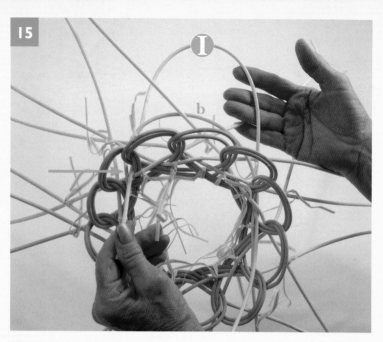

Now pick up "I" and follow along the inside of 'b' (see arrow) through the loop.

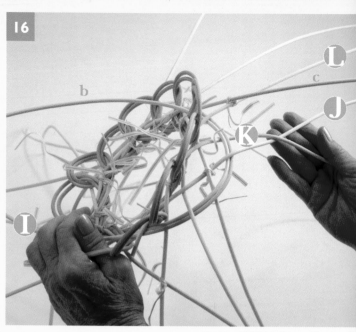

Strands "I" and 'b' are shown following each other from the previous step. Pick up strand 'c.' It will weave over strand "L", under strand "K", and over strand "J."

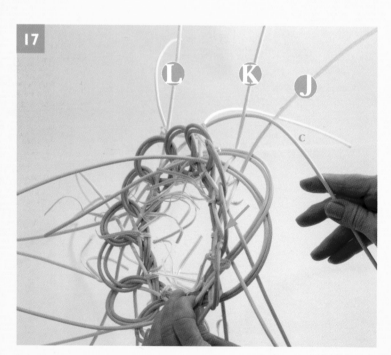

Strand 'c' then follows strand "J" into the loop. Pick up the next strand to the left and continue the process.

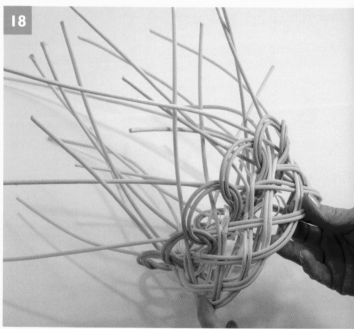

All of the pairs of strands have now been woven back into the center of the cycloid circle and the woven foot is completed.

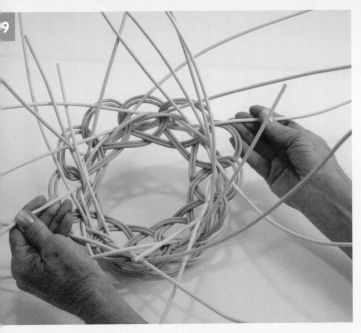

Looking into the center of the cycloid base, find the opposite ends of each pair of strands and pull, tug, and tighten until the foot is uniform under the cycloid disk.

When the base looks complete to you, trim the right facing strands just past their intersection with their left facing strand.

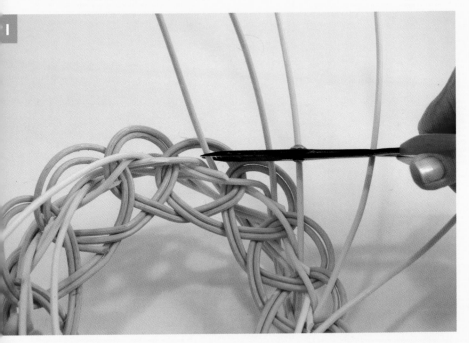

Now trim the left-facing strands just above where they emerge into view.

Set your gourd on the cycloid base through which you wove the foot. Place your second disk around the neck of the gourd. Adjust the disks until they both fit comfortably around the gourd and there is some space between the two disks. On one side of the gourd, use several twist ties to anchor the disks to each other so that they are still parallel to each other when viewed from the side. These anchors will keep the upper disk from changing position when we start lashing the disks together on the other side.

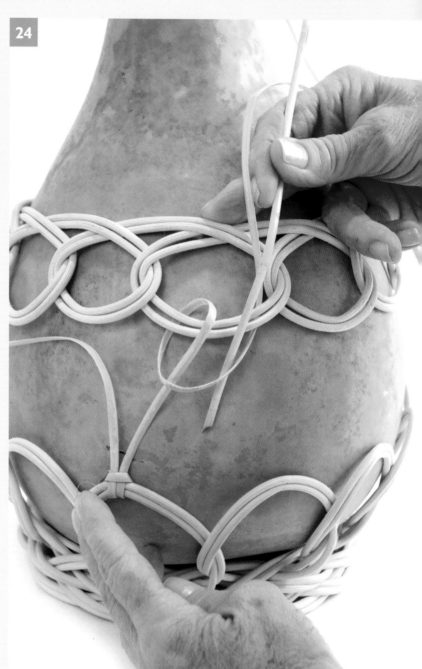

23

Turn the gourd around so the unanchored side is facing you. Adjust the disks so that the loops are offset from top to bottom.

24

Select a long length (20') of 4mm binder cane and attach it to one of the loops of the bottom cycloid disk. Bring one of the ends up to adjacent loop on the upper disk, go around the loop and come o to the left of the strand. Cross over the strand and go back into th same loop from behind. Bring the end through the loop formed b the cane.

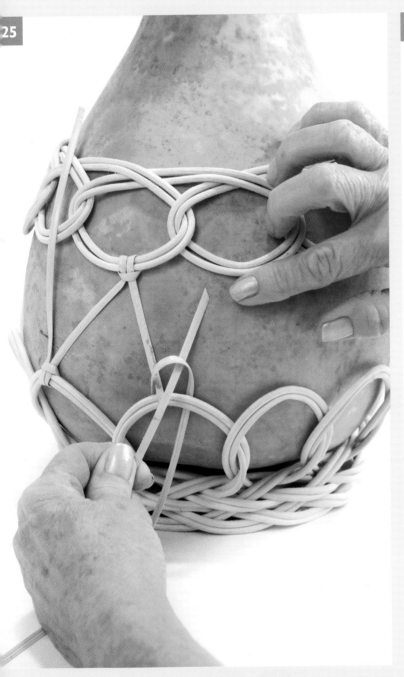

Carefully pull the loop taut and then bring the strand of cane down to the next loop on the bottom disk and repeat the process. It is important to keep the knots in the center of the reed loops.

Continue lashing the two disks together making sure the spacing between the two loops remains consistent and the disks remain parallel to each other.

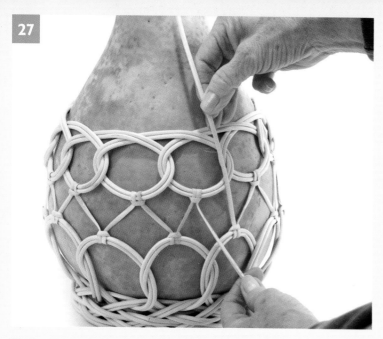

27

To finish the lashing, interweave the end of the strand with the first larks head knot to hide the ends.

28

To end the lashing strand you will double the first lark's head knot. Pass the finishing end through the loop made by the beginning end of the lashing strand.

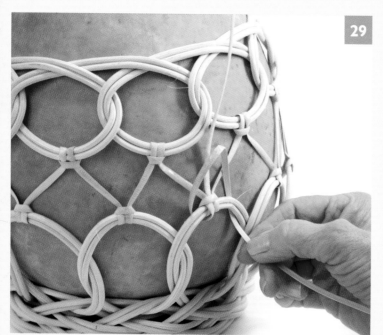

29

Bring the around the reed loop and back up to the left and then over the pair of strands from the starting loop and back down behind the reed loop.

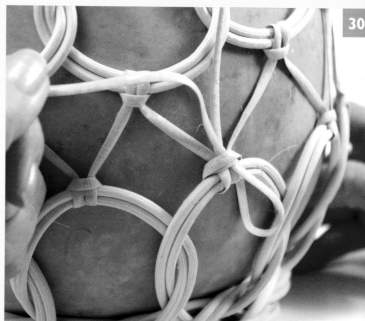

30

Bring the strand up through the loop just made which doubles the beginning loop. Pull the strand tight.

24

31

After making sure the new knot is secure, trim both loose ends flush with the knot.

2

Drill a 3/4" hole near the top of the gourd.

33

Tie the ends of the four 40" lengths of coconut fiber together and pass all four strands behind the top of the ring and out the loop in the ring.

34 Bring the four ends up and through the middle of the loop created by the knot at the end of the four strands.

35 Pull the knot tight and trim the four tails at the end of t[h]e knot. Braid the four strands together by passing the le[ft] hand strand behind two strands and back over one, a[nd] then passing the right-hand strand behind two strands a[nd] back over one. Repeat with the left-hand strand, then t[he] right-hand strand.

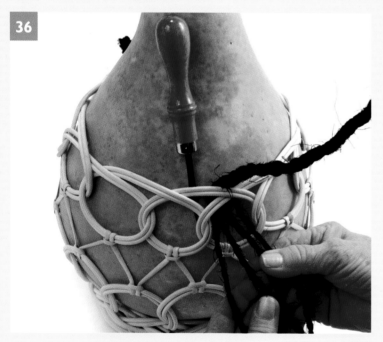

36 When the handle is long enough, pass all four strands behind the top of the ring and out the loop of the ring.

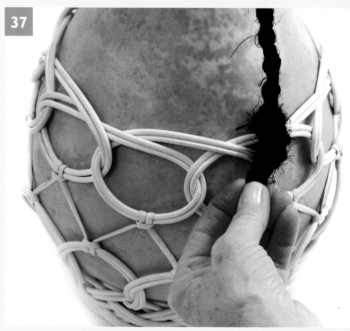

37 Tie an overhand knot around the hand, pull tight and tr[im] the ends.

BORNEO CYCLOID

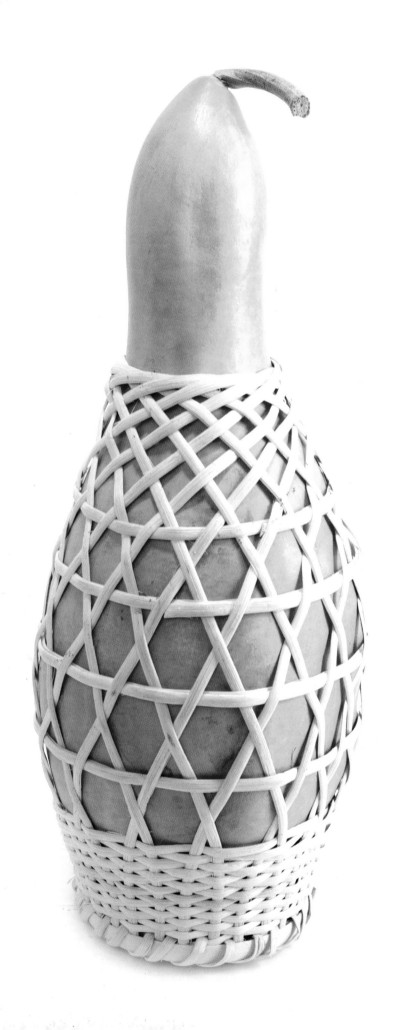

CHAPTER THREE

Malaysian Rinko Start

THIS weaving exercise begins at the neck of the gourd with the rinko woven start. Then the strands are plaited together for a few rows before the horizontal element in the triaxial weave begins. When the weaving elements are made vertical, we weave many rows of plain weaving, but with a 2 over 2 under twill to keep the weaving pattern correct. We finish the weaving with a traditional bamboo style foot which is most appropriate for use with flat weaving materials, allowing this tall, unwieldy gourd the ability to stand upright. This style of water bottle can be found throughout the Malaysian peninsula.

I strongly recommend practicing the Rinko start with paper strips until you feel very comfortable with it before you weave with the flat oval reed.

WHAT YOU'LL need

- 1 coil 1/4" flat oval reed
- 1 bottle gourd approximately 16" tall x 4" in diameter

WHAT YOU'LL do

- Soak the reed in hot water for 10 minutes. Remove from water and hang the strands so they dry straight. Cut 12 strands of 1/4" flat oval reed to 36" length.

- In steps 1 through 24, we've used strips of paper to more clearly indicate the order of the steps for creating the rinko start. In step 25, we switch to the flat oval reed to continue the project.

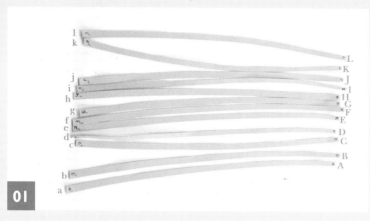

01

Cut 12 strands of 1/4 flat weaving elements, 36" in length. Label one end of the first strip "A" and the opposite end 'a.' Continue with the rest of the 11 strands, one end "B" the other 'b', and so on.

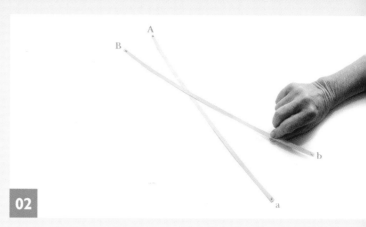

02

Place strand A as shown and then place strand B on top of A.

03

Place strand C on top of B and A.

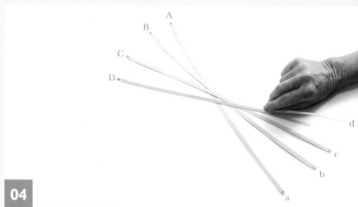

04

Place strand D on top of C, B, and A.

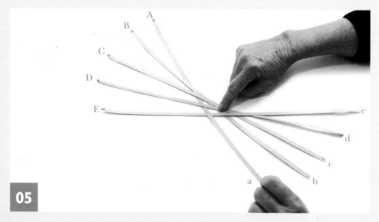

05

Lift 'a' and slide strand E under 'a' and on top of 'b', 'c', and 'd'.

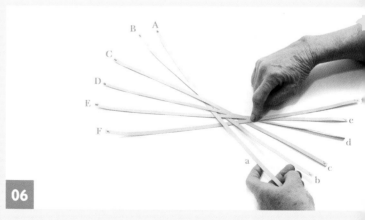

06

Lift Strand 'a' and 'b' and slide strand F under A and B, and on top of 'c', 'd', and 'e'.

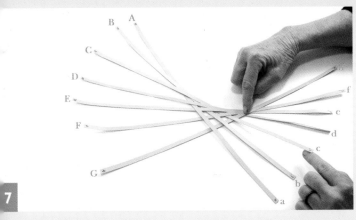

7

t 'a', 'b,' and 'c' and slide strand G under 'a', 'b', 'c', and
top of 'd', 'e,' and 'f'.

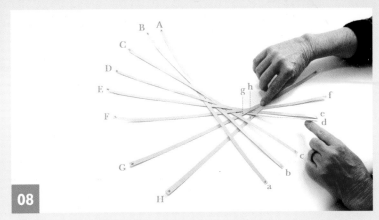

08

Continue by sliding H under 'a', 'b', 'c', and 'd', and over
'e', 'f', and 'g'.

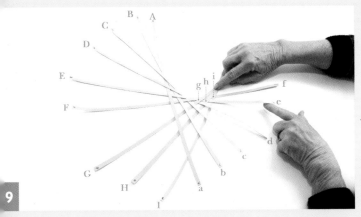

9

de I under 'a', 'b', 'c', 'd', and 'e' and over 'f', 'g', and 'h'.

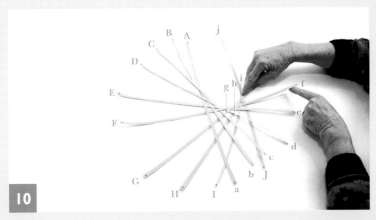

10

Slide J under 'b', 'c', 'd' , 'e', and 'f' and over 'g', 'h', and 'i'.

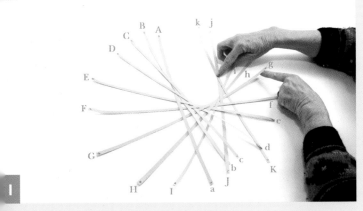

1

de K under 'e', 'f', 'g', and on top of 'h', 'i', and 'j'.

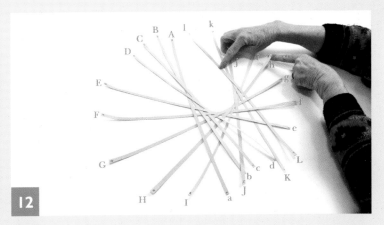

12

Slide L over 'e', under 'f', 'g', and 'h', and over 'i,' 'j', and 'k'.

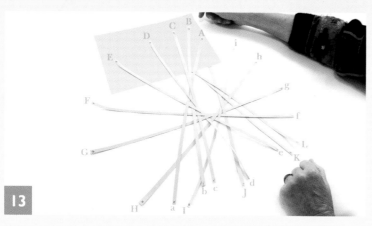

13 Before you interweave the ends into the beginning elements, slide a piece of paper in so that it is laying on top of 'j', 'k', and 'l'.

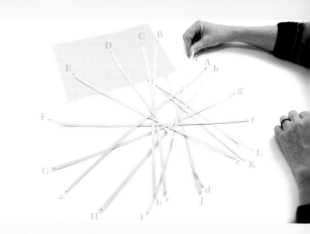

14 Lift 'i' and maneuver A under 'i'.

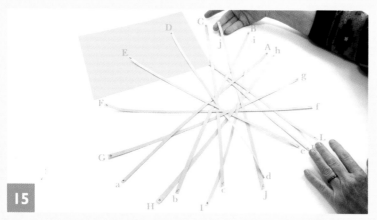

15 Lift 'j' and maneuver **B** under 'j'.

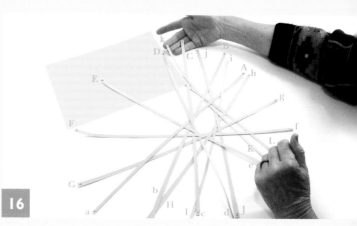

16 Lift 'k' and move C under 'k'.

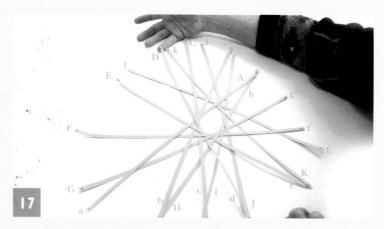

17 Lift 'l' and move **D** under 'l'.

18 Gently tighten up center by pushing the opposite corners together.

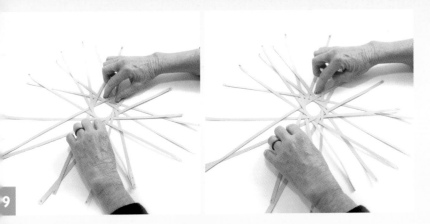

9

...ontinue gently tightening up center.

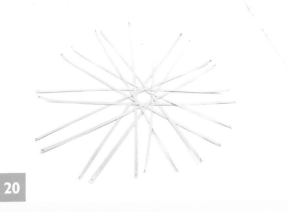

20

The completed Rinko start.

...ck up Rinko start with one hand and …

22

Place Rinko start over neck of gourd so that the gourd neck emerges from the center of the start.

...ently bring ends of the elements down around the gourd. ...et the gourd and the weaving elements in hot water for ...minutes. Bring the ends together at the bottom of the ...ourd and secure them with a rubber band so that they dry ...ainst the gourd.

24

Here are the 12 weaving elements the following day after drying to conform to the shape of the gourd.

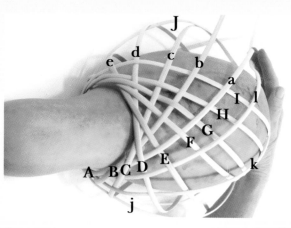

25

Study this weave of the next completed step. This is an over 1, under 1, over 1, under 1 weave. The strands facing to the left will be the working (or weaving) strands.

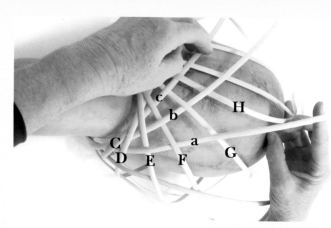

2

Strand 'a' emerges from under B, C, and D. Weave it ov E, under F, and over G. Weave strand 'b' over F, und G, and over H.

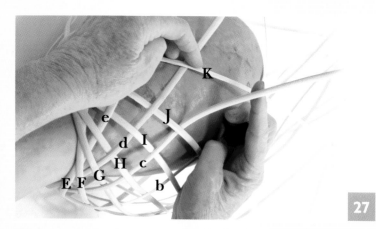

27

Weave strand 'c' over G, under H, over I, and under J and then weave strand 'd' over H, under I, and over J.

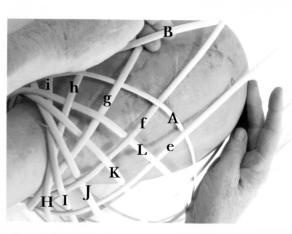

2

Weave 'e' over I, under J, over K, and under L. Weave over J, under K, over L, and under A. Weave 'g' over under L, over A, and under B. Continue the rest of the w around to the beginning.

29

Insert the first horizontal weaver by slipping the element under the diagonal weavers, weaving out to the right, and over the diagonal weavers, weaving out to the left.

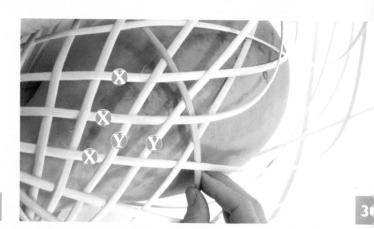

3

The horizontal weave will weave over row 'Y' and under row 'X.'

31

32

ter the horizontal row intersects with **X** and **Y**, bring **Y** top of **X** to lock the horizontal row.

The lock is complete.

33

34

y in the 2nd horizontal row as before. It will be easier to see ith this row. The horizontal row will be under the diagonal ements that are weaving up to the right (**X**) and over the agonal elements that are weaving up to the left (**Y**).

After weaving under **X** and over **Y**, lock the horizontal into place by placing **Y** over **X**. Lock the two diagonal elements after each intersection with the horizontal element.

35

36

verlap the two ends of each horizontal row and weave ross several intersections to hold the weave in place. Pull each end to tighten the weave against the gourd.

The gourd is upside down. Determine where the base of the weave should be and straighten the diagonal elements into vertical elements for the last weaving step.

37

38

Weave an under one, over one, under one pattern using the diagonal elements as parallel vertical elements. In order to keep the weave progressing upwards, a pair of vertical elements is crossed each time around (shown in pink) resulting in a twill weave.

Trim the ends 8" above the last row of weaving.

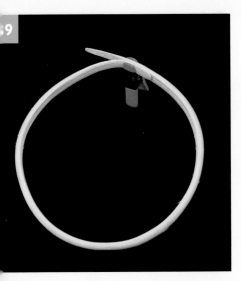

etermine the diameter of the base and
ake a rim of 1/2" split round reed by
rming the split round reed into a circle
nd gluing the two ends together.

it rim piece around the weaving,
utside of the vertical spokes. Fold
ne of the vertical elements (spoke)
owards the inside of the weaving and
nder and around the rim.

41

Bring the element up around the rim and through the loop that was formed.

Bring the next spoke to the right in towards the center of the weaving, around the tail piece from the previous spoke, and under and through the rim.

Bring the end up around the rim and through the loc it formed. (The loop now contains two ends.)

ring the next spoke to the right around both ends, under
nd through the rim.

Bring the end up around the rim and into the loop formed.
(The loop now contains 3 ends.)

Continue as before all the way around the base of the weaving. Bring the fourth spoke around the last 2 of the ends and wrap under the rim and back through the loop. (This loop only contains the most recent 3 ends.)

47

Keep dropping one end as you progress while adding the newest end to the group. The last spoke will loop over 2 ends and finish in its loop.

48

Pull all the ends snug until the base feels firm and symmetrical. Trim each end where it emerges from its last loop.

MALAYSIAN RINKO START

The finished project.

CHAPTER FOUR

Mexican Netted Water Bule

WHAT YOU'LL need

MAGUEY is the traditional plant from which Central American craftsmen prepare sisal, for spinning and twisting into cordage and ropes. With the prepared cordage it is a simple matter to quickly knot a net around a gourd for carrying water for a workday in the sun. This project is a simple example for turning any gourd into a convenient water bottle or canteen. As the water slowly evaporates through the skin of the gourd, heat is drawn from the water in the gourd to convert the liquid evaporate into a vapor, thus cooling the water in the gourd well below the ambient temperature, just as perspiration cools the face.

- Large gourd
- Corn cob
- Spool of Sisal cordage
- Two strands of cordage 120" long
- Fourteen strands of cordage 108" long

01

Drill a 3/4" hole in the neck of the gourd where you want the drinking or pouring spout to be. Fill the gourd with ho[...] water and hang it upright so that the water will percolate through the neck into the large reservoir. This might take a fe[...] days. After several days, or as long as a week, pour out some of the water, vigorously shake the gourd and then spill o[...] the rest of the water.

02

After soaking the inside of the gourd for a week, the plug still wasn't dissolved so we purchased a new plumber's snake and unblocked the plug between the neck and the reservoir of the gourd. Once the plug was dissolved, we filled the gourd with hot water, added some 3/4" metal washers and gravel, vigorously shook the gourd, and poured out the contents. This process was repeated until we were sure the gourd was thoroughly cleaned out.

03

Cut a section of the corn cob and carve the end of th[...] cob until it fits the hole in the neck of the gourd.

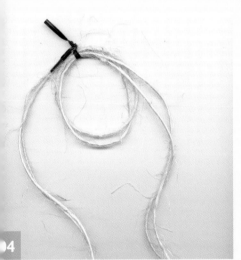

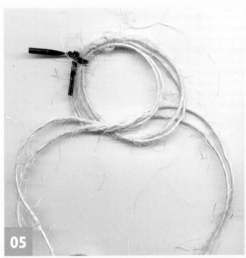

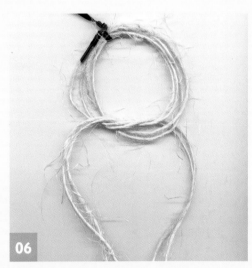

04 ~~vo~~ strands of cordage, 120" long. Fold ~~in~~ half and make full loop with both ~~co~~rds. Use a twist tie at to top of the ~~lo~~op to keep midpoint from slipping.

05 Tie half of a square knot with the 4 ends and slip one pair of ends behind the loop and the pair in front of the loop.

06 Adjust the knot so that the loops are aligned. The diameter of the loop must be smaller than the bottom diameter of the gourd.

07

Tie an overhand knot with all four strands as one below the loop.

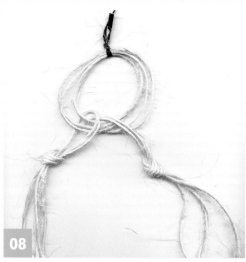

08

Find the center of two 108" strands and loop them over the central loop. Tie an overhand knot with all four strands the same distance from the central loop as in the previous step.

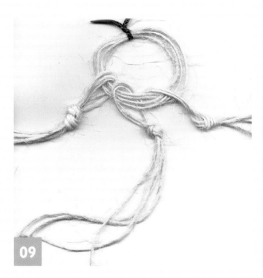

09

Find the midpoint of the next pair of 108" strands and thread them around the central loop. Tie an overnight knot using all 4 strands as with the previous two groups.

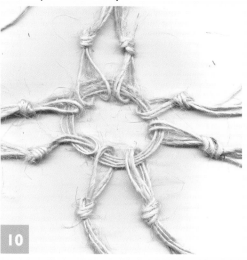

10

Continue as before until 8 sets of double strands are tied to the central loop.

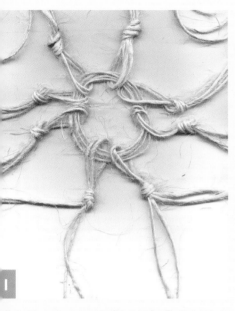

11 ...ck up two strands each from two ...jacent sets of strands.

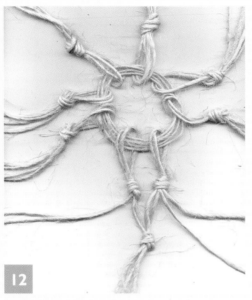

12 Tie an overhand knot with these two pairs of strands.

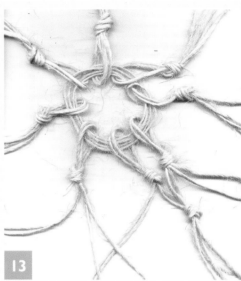

13 Pick up the pair of strands left over and pair them with two strands from the adjacent set to the left.

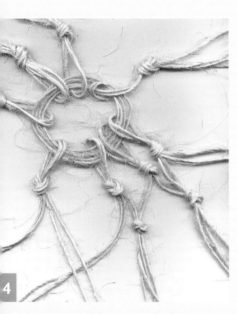

14 ...e an overhand knot with these two ...irs of strands. Pick up the next pair ...strands.

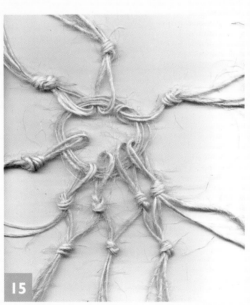

15 The third knot completed. The left over 2 strands are visible on the left.

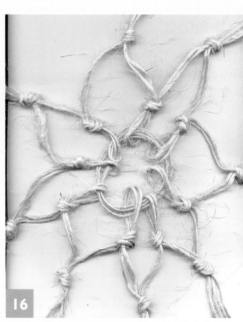

16 Continue until all 8 knots of the second row are completed.

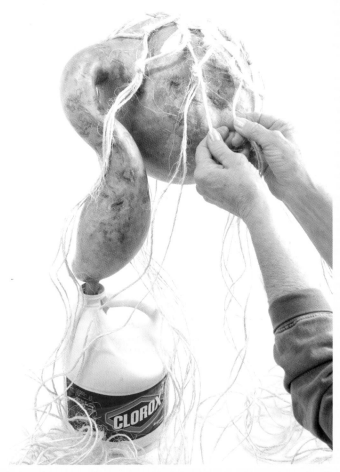

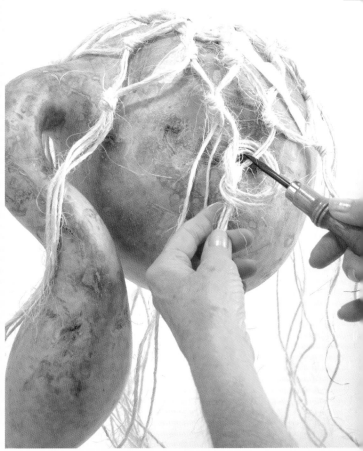

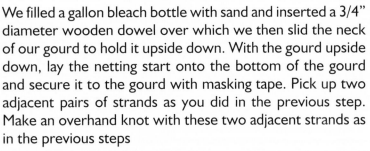

We filled a gallon bleach bottle with sand and inserted a 3/4" diameter wooden dowel over which we then slid the neck of our gourd to hold it upside down. With the gourd upside down, lay the netting start onto the bottom of the gourd and secure it to the gourd with masking tape. Pick up two adjacent pairs of strands as you did in the previous step. Make an overhand knot with these two adjacent strands as in the previous steps

You can control exactly where your knot will lay in the n by using an awl or fid. Place the tip of the fid through th upper loop of the overhand knot, touch the tip to the gou and tighten the knot.

Pick up the adjacent two pairs of strands and continue makin overhand knots all the way around the gourd. Continue th rows of overhand netting knots until the netting is abov the top of the gourd.

20

21

om the 32 individual strands, gather adjacent pairs and ist them together into 16 strands of 2ply cordage. Twist e two individual plies counter-clockwise between your gers and thumb.

Then twist the left-hand ply over the right-hand ply and change hands. The twisting of the two plies together in the opposite direction that the individual plies were twisted, keeps the cordage intact.

22

23

hen all 16 strands of 2-ply cordage are finished lift up the nds to separate and straighten the strands.

Gather all 16 sisal strands together into three groups; 5 strands each in two groups and 6 strands in the third group.

Groups 1 and 2 will attach to the netting on either side of group 3. Group 3, after braiding with groups 1 and 2 will attach to the netting between gourds 1 and 2. Tie the ends of group 1 together around the top of the net on one side of group 3. Tie the ends of group 2 to the other side of group 3.

Starting at the base of Group 3, bring the str made up Group 1 on the left and over Group Bring Group 3 over Group 1 and under Group Now cross Group 1 over Group 2. Bring Grou 3 over Group 1 and under Group 2. Contin braiding the three groups of strands togeth tightening and adjusting the braid as you progre When there is no more room to braid any furth tie the end of the single group to the netted b by untying the knot at the end of the group a tying off several strands at a time to different par of the netted bag. Untie the knotted group at t beginning of the braid and distribute the individu strands in smaller groups as you knot this end the netted bag.

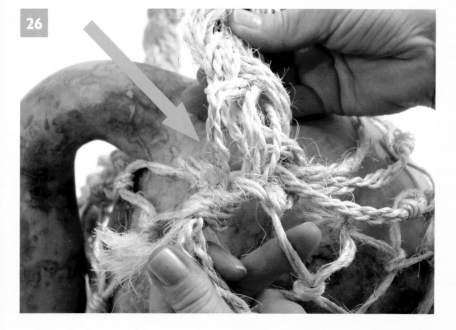

When there is no more room to braid any furthe tie the end of the single group to the netted ba (blue arrow).

The finished netted water gourd carrier with the corn cob stopper.

CHAPTER FIVE

Hawaiian Netting

WHAT YOU'LL need

The Hawaiians are sailors first and foremost and carrying fresh water is imperative on long ocean voyages. Being able to keep your gourd canteen handy, yet secure, meant good knot tying and netting knowledge would come into play. Simplicity and elegance are the hallmarks of a good sailor.

- 50 feet of braided cord
- Masking tape
- Conical shell for stopper
- Drill

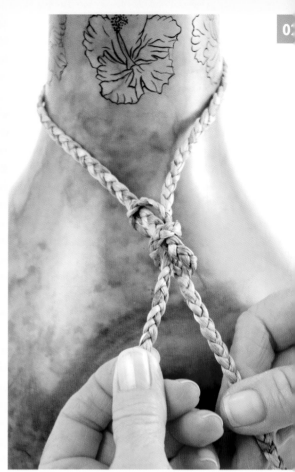

02

Prepared gourd was sanded and embellished with woodburning and color; 24' of braided abaca and assorted shells to choose for stopper.

Bring the braided cord around the neck and t[...]
an overhand or slipknot so that the loop arour[...]
the neck can be adjusted.

Tighten the knot so that the loop lies slightly belo[...]
the final placement of the loop. As the netting [...]
woven, the tension in the loop will tighten.

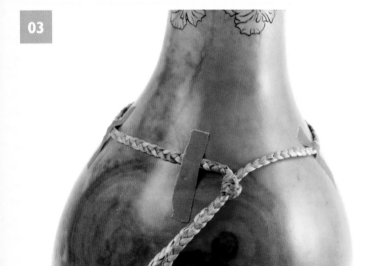

03

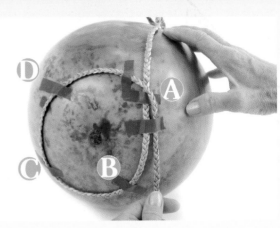

04

...ing the long length of cordage to the bottom of the gourd ...d form a clockwise circle around the bottom. Use masking ...pe to hold the circle at 4 corners.

05

Bring the cordage over the starting point **A** of the circle and begin a 2nd time around. Tape the 2nd circle as you go around the outside of the first circle.

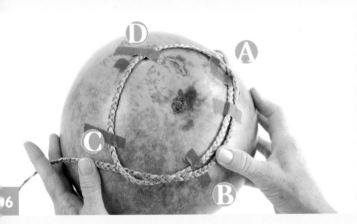

06

...fter you pass the 2nd corner **B**, go over the first circle and ...en pass the cordage back under the first circle before you ...ach the 3rd corner **C**.

07

After you pass the 4th corner **D**, go over and then under the first circle. Bring the cordage just past the corner and interweave by passing under the first circle and then over the 2nd circle.

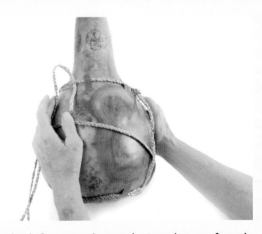

08

...ross the cordage under the strand coming down from ...e neck.

09

Bring the strand to the left, up to the neck ring about a fourth of the way around the neck from the knot on the ring.

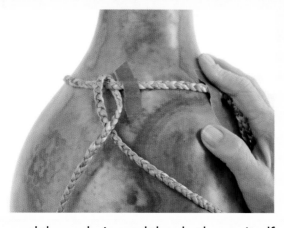

10

Go over and around the neck ring and then back over itself to the left.

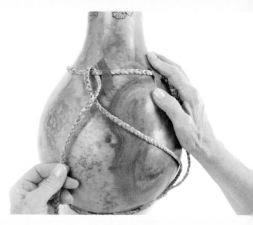

11

Continuing the movement to the left, bring the cordage back down to the circle on the bottom.

12

Interweave the cordage with the base ring by passing over the 2nd ring and under the first ring at **D**, then back up to the left over the inner ring and under the outer ring.

13

Bring the cordage up to the neck ring about halfway around from the knot on the neck ring. Pass over and around the neck ring and then pass over itself to the left (as pictured).

14

Interweave the cordage to the bottom rings at **C**. Pass the cordage back up to the neck ring and over itself to the left as in the previous step. Then bring the cordage back down to the bottom double ring and interweave at **B**. Bring the cordage back up toward the neck ring.

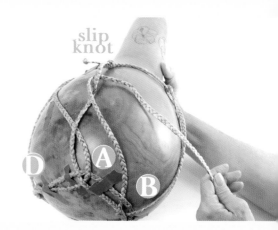

15

Instead of bringing the cordage all the way to the neck ring in this step, pass the strand over and around the strand as it left the slip knot and bring it to the right.

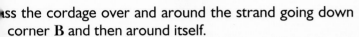

6

ass the cordage over and around the strand going down corner **B** and then around itself.

17

Pull the loop around the two strands taut and then pass the cordage under and over the 3rd neck ring loop.

8

ontinue to the right and pass the cordage around the next vo strands associated with corner **C**.

19

Go under and over the 2nd neck ring loop and continue to the right.

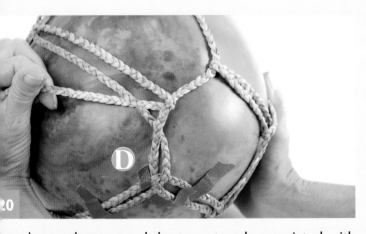

20

ass the cordage around the two strands associated with orner **D**.

21

Pass the cordage through the loop of the two strands associated with corner **A**.

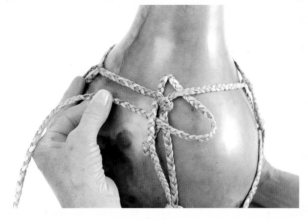

22

Bring the cordage up to the left of the slipknot and make a loop under the net ring. Bring the end of the cordage over the strand coming from the slipknot and then under itself. Do not pull the loop tight.

23

Interweave the strand with the 3 loops around the neck rir and then around the slipknot. Adjust and tighten the cordag throughout the entire netting on the gourd and when it looks symmetrical and beautiful, tighten the knot.

24

Bring the remaining end of the cord up and over the top of the gourd.

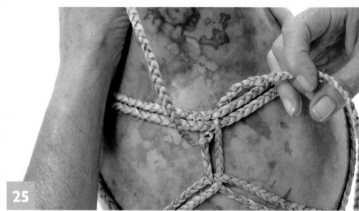

25

Bring the cord down to the opposite side of the gourd fro the last knot you tied and slip the end between the pa of vertical strands and behind the double row that passe around the neck of the gourd.

26

After passing the cord back across the top of the gourd and around the beginning side of the handle, adjust the length of the doubled handle until the length seems right. The gourd should hang upright when suspended.

27

To begin the knotted handle, make a 3" loop in the leftove handle cord.

Find the very middle of the handle and make a loop that begins 1-1/2 inches before the middle and ends 1-1/2 inches after the middle.

eginning at the bottom of the loop, tightly wrap the cord round both parts of the handle and also around the loop everal times and finally pass the end through the loop and ull tight.

egin wrapping around the two parts of the handle and the op as you did with the previous knot.

Make the third knot to cover the last 3 inches of the handle. Tie an overhand knot in the end of the cord one or two inches beyond this last knot. Then trim the cord just beyond this knot.

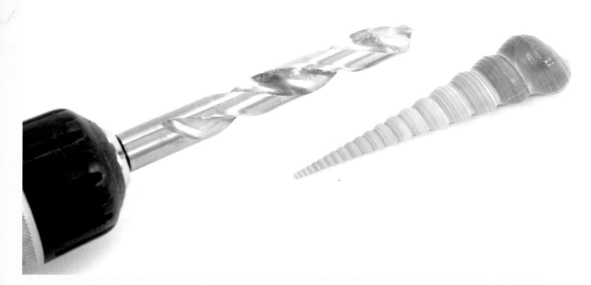

A 3/8" drill bit is approximately the same diameter as the middle of this auger shell.

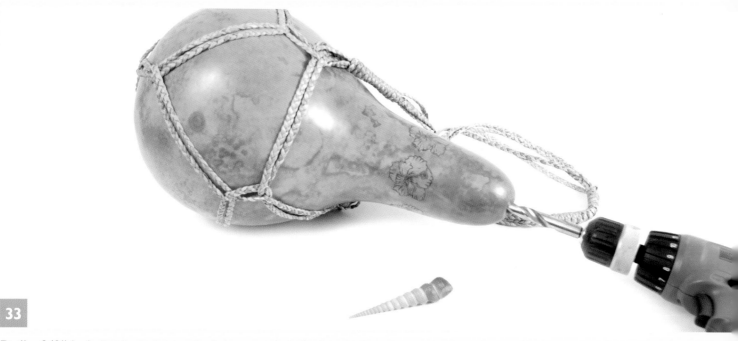

33

Drill a 3/8" hole in the stem end of the gourd to fit the shell stopper.

The completed
Hawaiian netted gourd
water bottle.

CHAPTER SIX

Hexagonal Spiral

I first learned Hebi Kago from a Japanese basketry artist who taught at The Caning Shop in the early 1980s. This weave makes a very quick ikebana basket as well as an elegant packaging. Weaving around a gourd with this simple hexagonal technique adds texture and interest — whether the gourd is holding water for drinking or a flower stem.

WHAT YOU'LL need

- 8 strands of 1/4" flat oval reed cut to 36"

- Dye: orange, dark blue, yellow, dark green, black, red, purple, brown (each strand should be dyed one of these colors)

- 1 strand of 1/4" flat oval reed cut to 15' left natural color

- 9-12 miniature spring clamps

- 1 club or snake gourd approximately 3-1/2" diameter x 12" tall

- 3 long weights (18" spokeweight, heavy rulers, steel bars)

WHAT YOU'LL do

- Dye the 8 strands with leather dye, magic markers, or other coloring material.

- Soak the 9 strands in hot water (~100°F) for no more than 10-15 minutes.

01

Find the midpoint of each colored strand of 1/4" flat oval reed. Lay the orange strand on the table and, at its midpoint, cross it on top with the dark blue strand.

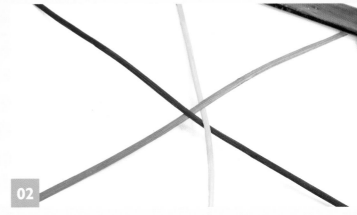

02

Insert the midpoint of the yellow strand under and to the rig of the orange strand and on top of the dark blue strand.

03

Insert the midpoint of the green strand under the dark blue strand and over the yellow strand and to the right of the yellow strand.

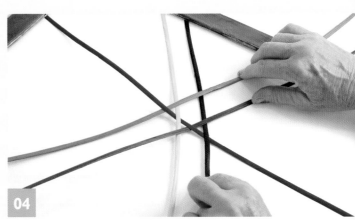

04

Insert the midpoint of the black strand under the oran strand and under the green strand, to the right of intersection with the dark blue strand, and over the da blue strand.

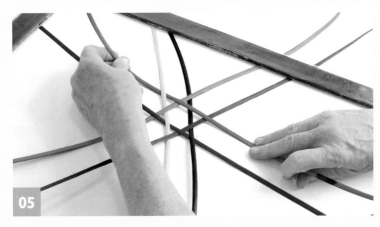

05

Insert the midpoint of the red strand under the yellow strand and over the orange strand, to the right of the intersection of the yellow and orange strands, and over the black strand and over the green strand.

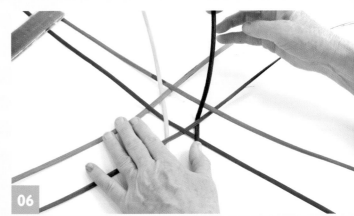

06

Lift the black strand from under the orange and red strand

8 @ 36" Orange, blue, yellow, green, (black) red
pink green purple
Pink?

64

olonge, blue, yellow, pink, green purple red, sky blue

HEXAGONAL SPIRAL

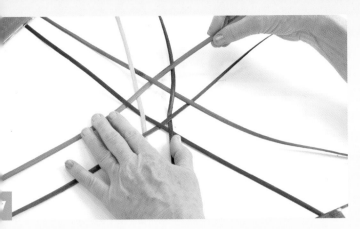

y the end of the black strand over the red strand and under
e orange strand. This will "lock" the black and orange
ands and secure the red strand into place.

This "lock" will be used constantly throughout this project.
Insert the midpoint of the purple strand under the orange
and green strands and over the red and blue strands. Weight
the ends.

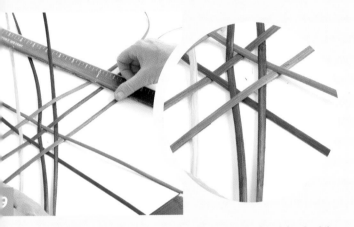

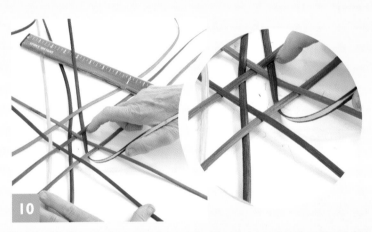

y the midpoint of the brown strand over the black, blue,
d purple strands and under the red strand. Slide the end
der the weight to help anchor it.

Lift the end of the purple strand back, and slip the blue
strand on top of the brown strand.

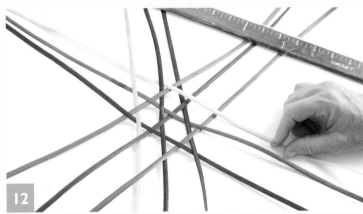

y the purple strand on top of the blue strand.

Lay the weight on top of the yellow, black, purple, orange,
green, and brown strands. Take the natural colored strand
and slip a tail of 18" under the black and yellow strands, and
place the rest of the strand on top of the orange, purple,
green, and brown strands.

purple grey
red skyblue

HEXAGONAL SPIRAL

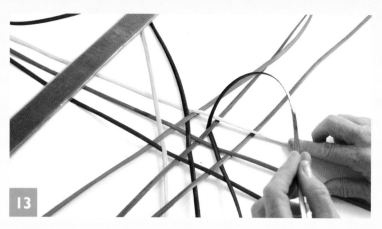

13 Fold the purple strand back to its intersection with the green strand.

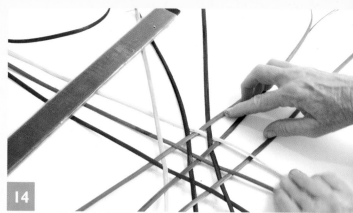

14 Slip the purple strand back over the natural strand and "loc[k] it under the orange strand.

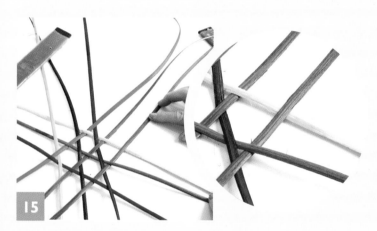

15 Slide the natural strand under the brown strand.

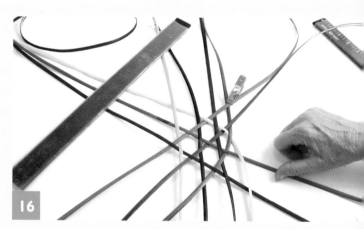

16 Lock the green strand over the orange strand. Clamp t[he] brown and orange strands together. Ease the natural stra[nd] over the red and blue strands as shown.

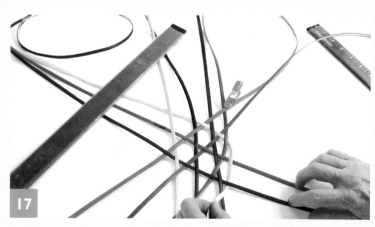

17 Slide the natural strand under the blue strand and over the purple strand.

18 Bring the blue strand over the red strand and clam[p] their intersection.

19 ...ing the natural strand over the purple strand and under ...e black strand. Clamp the intersection of the black and ...rple strands.

20 Bring the natural strand over the brown strand and under the yellow strand. "Lock" the brown strand over the yellow strand and clamp their intersection.

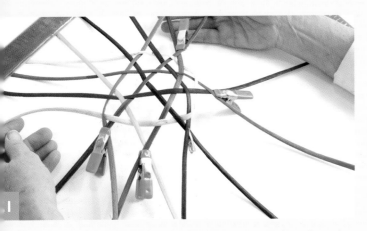

21 ...ing the natural strand over the green strand and under ...e orange strand. Then "lock" the green strand over the ...ange strand and clamp their intersection.

22 Bring the natural strand over the blue strand and under the red strand. "Lock" the blue strand over the red strand and clamp their intersection.

23 ...ring the natural strand over the yellow strand and under ...e short end of the natural strand. "Lock" the short end ...f the natural strand under the yellow strand and clamp ...eir intersection.

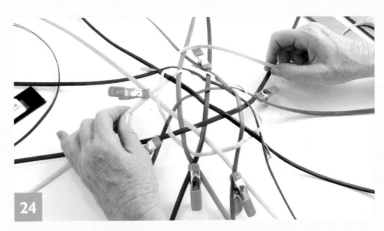

24 Continue by bringing the natural strand over the black strand and under the purple strand. "Lock" the black strand over the purple strand and clamp their intersection.

25

Bring the natural strand over the orange strand and under the brown strand. "Lock" the orange strand over the brown strand and clamp their intersection.

Begin forming the weaving into a bowl shape to fit over the base of the gourd. The next intersection will be with the green and blue strands. Bring the natural strand over the green strand and under the blue strand. "Lock" the green strand over the blue strand and clamp their intersection.

27

Slip the weaving over the flower end of the gourd. The next intersection will be with the red and black strands.

28

Bring the natural strand over the red strand and under the black strand. "Lock" the red strand over the black strand. Continue this pattern of weaving around and around the gourd.

29

Bring all of the ends together.

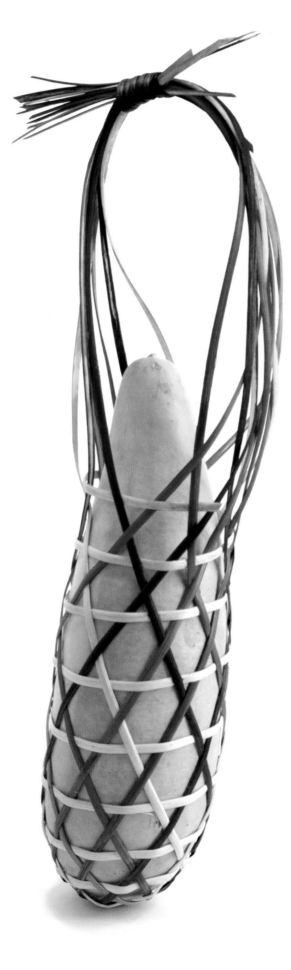

The finished project
with all the ends
tied together.

- 1 Gourd, 8-10 inches in diameter x 12-16 inches tall

- Masking Tape

- #3 Round Reed (2.25mm) 20'

- 11/64" Flat Oval Reed 1/4 lb.

- 3/8" or 1/2" Flat Reed

- 12-1/2" flat oval reed

For the Base

- 1/4" Flat Reed or Splint

- 20' of 1/4" flat reed dyed red

- 6' 1-1/4" Ash splint, cedar bark, hickory bark, palm bark

- Masking Tape

Tools Needed

- Nippers or sharp shears

- Fid or tapered awl

- Round nose pliers

- Ruler, Spray bottle, and water source

CHAPTER SEVEN

Cameroon Palm Wine Bottle

do

The shell of the gourd should be clean with all of the outer skin, mold, and dirt removed. If this is to be made into a water or wine bottle, the gourd will need to be opened and completely cleaned and washed to remove any bitter taste from the gourd.

Round and Flat Oval Reeds should be soaked in hot water for only a few minutes. Over-soaking causes the reed to become hairy, brittle, and to change color.

Keep the hoop moist, not sopping wet, while weaving. You can remove the reeds from the soaking tub and place them into a plastic bag to keep them moist while weaving. When you stop working, allow everything to dry out completely and then rewet them when you come back to work.

I found the original Palm Wine Bottle from Cameroon on ebay. The seller had it with her Chianti bottles in their home bar. I recognized it immediately from When Art Shares Nature's Gift — The African Calabash and was overjoyed to see it in person. It sat with me for several years before I finally got up the courage to weave a reproduction. There were many, many lessons to learn about the order in which to approach this task — and there were many false starts. However, we succeeded and can only be in awe of the artistry that was required to design this bottle.

The weaving pattern used for the entire hoop is a Figure Eight and woven in two steps. The first step is the upper loop of the figure eight going from right to left, over the round reed on the right and under the round reed on the left, and then through the hoop to the right. The second step is the lower loop of the figure eight going from right to left, under the round reed on the right and over the round reed on the left, and then through the hoop to the right.

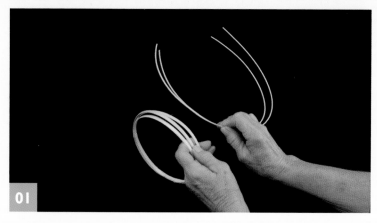

01

02

Make a hoop with a 5' length of 11/64" flat oval reed. Go around 3 times to make the hoop 5-5.5" in diameter. Use masking tape to hold the ends together. Have beginning and end of hoop end at same location to keep thickness of hoop uniform. Cut two pieces of #3 Round Reed, 20" in length. Use masking tape to attach them to the outside of the hoop. Leave a space between them.

Pick up a long length of 11/64" flat oval reed. Starting wi 4" tail on the right, lay the end of the flat oval reed, roun side up, over the round reed on the right and under round reed on the left, and then back through the hoo

03

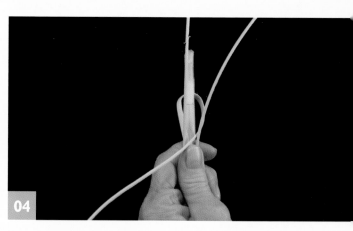

04

Slide the flat oval up to the left until you have the 4" tail below your left thumb. Bring the longer end of the flat oval reed to the left and through the hoop to the right.

Bring the end of the flat oval reed under the round re on the right and over the round reed on the left and th around and behind the arch of the hoop.

05

06

Bring the strand around and over the round reed on the right, over the previous passing of the flat oval reed, and under the round reed on the left.

As before, pass the flat oval reed around and through hoop to the right, returning under the round reed on right and over the round reed on the left.

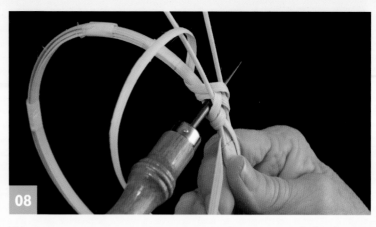

...ring the flat oval reed through the hoop and then over the ...ound reed on the right and under the round reed on the ...ft, and then through the hoop to the right. Then bring the ...at oval reed through the hoop and under the round reed ...n the right and over the round reed on the left.

We have now set up the pattern of weaving of the hoop. Use your Fid or tapered awl to make an insertion from the left between the two flat oval strands below and the two flat oval strands above, under the round reed strands but above the flat oval hoop.

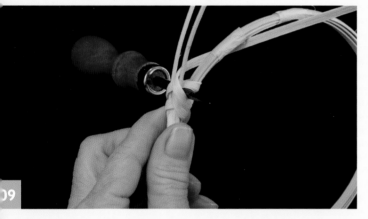

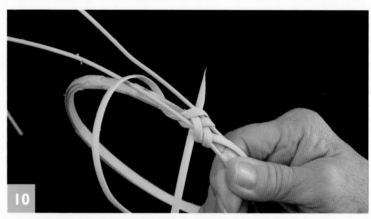

...he Fid or tapered awl should exit on the right side, just ...elow the top flat oval strand. Twist the Fid to open the ...ace between the plies of the braid, between the round ...ed strands and the flat oval hoop.

Remove the Fid and insert the end of the long flat oval strand through the space made by the Fid from the left to the right. It might help if you "point" the end of the strand before inserting it into the braid.

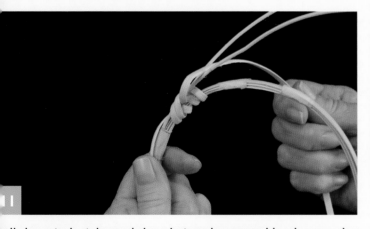

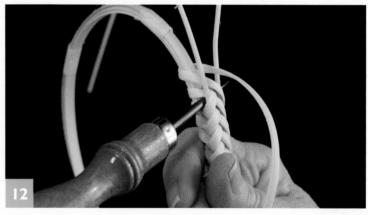

...ull the stitch tight and then bring the strand back over the ...ound reed on the right and under the round reed on the ...ft as you wove before.

This is now the repeating pattern. Bring the flat oval strand from behind under the round reed on the right. Insert the Fid below the two flat oval strands, between the round reed and hoop.

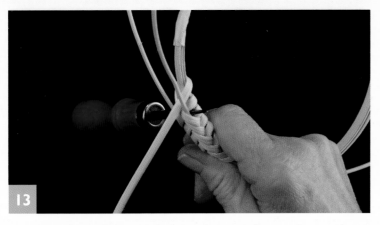

The tip of the Fid exits below the two flat oval strands on the right. This should be the adjacent loop from which the previous step exited.

At some point you will run out of your weaving strand. Splicing is easy.

Insert the Fid from the side opposite of the end of the strand. The Fid should parallel and be under the ending strand.

Twist, then remove the Fid and insert a new strand, oval side up, from the left to the right, under the ending strand.

Pull the new strand through the weave until only 1-2" of the tail is visible. Pull the tip of the ending strand tight and then trim the end at the edge of the hoop.

Continue weaving as before until you have approximately 2" of hoop still to cover. Now we will join the cut ends of the two strands of #3 Round Reed

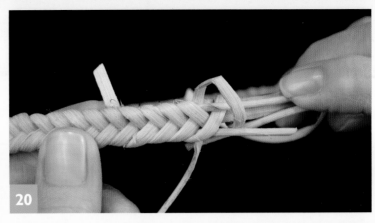

Start with one strand of Round Reed (here the one on the left-top in the photo). Trim one end with a long bias cut. Then trim the meeting end with a matching bias cut.

Here the two trimmed ends are visible under the open loop of flat oval reed. The two ends will be covered and anchored by the open loop of the braid. No glue is necessary.

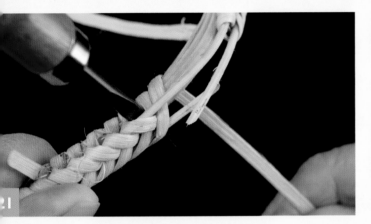

Insert the Fid into the next stitch of the weave, but carefully twist it so as not to release the end of the round reed. If the reed does come loose, just insert it back under the previous strand where it belongs.

Here is the splice of the round reed on the right, just above the tip of the Fid. The splice will be covered by the next stitch, which will go over the round reed on the right and under the round reed on the left.

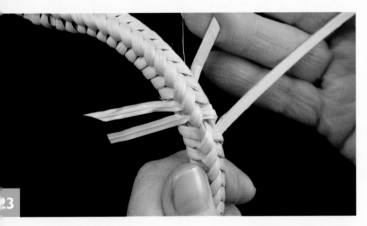

There is now only space for two more stitches. The two plastic twist tie lengths mark how the end of the braid will interweave with the two extra stitches from the beginning.

The next to the last stitch… Insert the end of the flat oval reed over the round reed on the right and through the stitch and under the round reed on the left.

Insert the Fid from the left in the same position as you have been doing. Now pull the stitch tight.

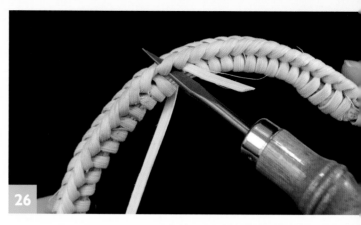

The last stitch... Insert the Fid from the right, through th stitch, and under the round reed on the right and over t round reed on the left. Twist and remove the Fid and inse the weaving strand.

For the 2nd half of the stitch, insert the Fid into the stitch by going over the round reed on the right and under the round reed on the left. Twist and remove the Fid and insert the weaving strand.

To hide the end of the weaving strand, once more inse the Fid into the next stitch by going under the round ree but on top of the earlier weaving strand.

Twist and remove the Fid and insert the weaving strand into the space. Pull the stitch tight and trim the end of the weaving strand as close as possible.

Slide the completed woven hoop around a bottle, jar, ca or tapered snake gourd (above) of the same diameter s that it will dry in a perfect circle.

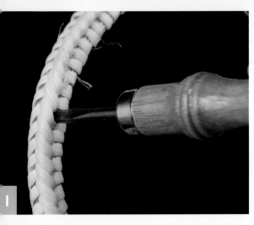

1

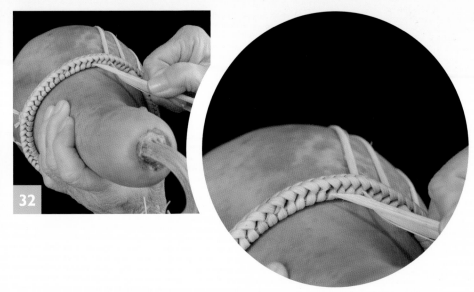

32

To lash the woven hoop to the gourd wine bottle, we will be lashing between the round reed and the 3-layer flat oval reed hoop. Use the Fid to make a space for the lashing strand.

Slip the hoop over the neck of the gourd and insert the flat oval reed lashing strand through the space made by the Fid.

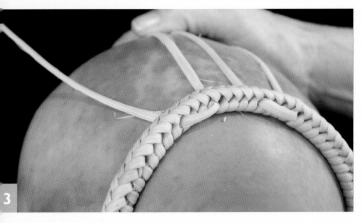

3

The spacing between the vertical lashing strands is 4 stitches. Every fourth stitch we'll insert the Fid, twist, and remove.

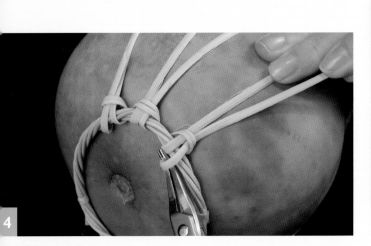

4

On the bottom of the gourd we have made a hoop out of several rounds a single length of #3 Round Reed, to which we are connecting the lashing strands with the larks head knot. Use the round nose pliers to adjust and tighten the knot. We have used long twist ties to temporarily hold the two rings in their proper placement so that as we tighten the lashing the rings will not move.

35

The gourd wine bottle showing the reed lashing on the left and the twist-tie lashing on the right.

36

To splice a new lasher, finish the larks head knot on the bottom ring.

37

Insert the new strand through the loop of the last larks head kn[ot] and tie another knot with the ends going through both loops

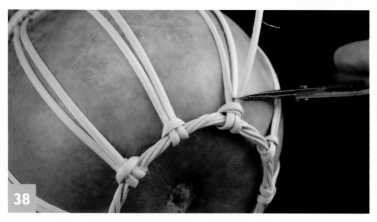

38

End the lashing strand in the first larks head knot in the same way as the splice. Trim the ends flush with the knot.

39

The two rings are lashed together.

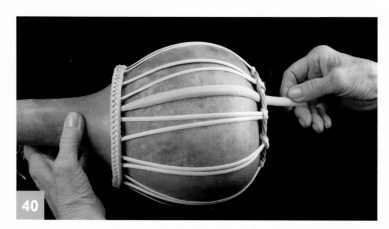

40

Insert a 12" length of 1/2" flat oval reed in the space between [the] [p]airs of lashing strands. The end of the reed on the left [i]s [?] inserted into the ring. The end on the [right ?] the bottom ring.

41

Take a new strand of 11/64" flat oval reed and insert or[e] end under the first lasher to the right of the wide flat ov[al] reed. Use the Fid or awl to lift the lashing strand.

42

ring the rest of the strand over the wide flat oval, make
loop of the 11/64" flat oval and insert the loop under the
ide strand and under the first lashing strand. Use the Fid
awl to lift the lashing strand.

43

Make another loop with the 11/64" flat oval and insert it
over the wide flat oval and under the lashing strand. Make
another loop and insert it under the wide flat oval and under
the lashing strand. Make a 4th loop.

44

ake a 5th loop. This loop will go under the wide flat oval
nd under the lashing strand.

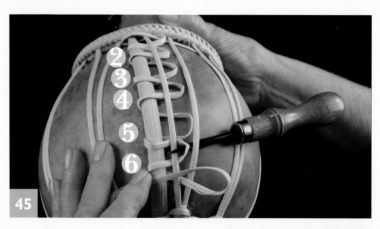

45

The 6th loop will go over the wide flat oval strand and
under the lashing strand. We have been making the loops
in a downward direction up to now. Now make a new loop
with the end of the strand directed up. Insert the Fid or awl
under the lashing strand to the right and through the 6th
loop from below and over the first lashing strand.

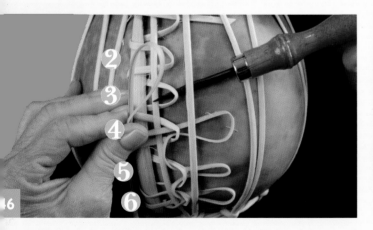

46

sert the new loop through the 6th loop from above and
der the 2nd lashing strand. Make another loop and insert
into the 5th loop from above and under the 2nd lashing
rand. Make another loop and insert it through the 4th loop
d under the 2nd lashing strand. Make another loop.

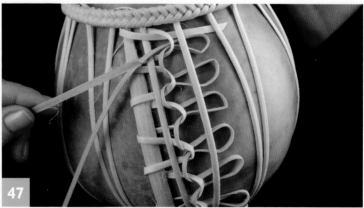

47

To begin the next column, make a loop with the strand
coming out of the first loop. Insert the new loop under the
2nd lashing strand, through the top loop and under the 3rd
lashing strand.

48

Continue making loops, inserting them through the loop in the 2nd column and under the 3rd lashing strand. Keep the intersection of the loops in the middle of each column. Constantly adjust the tension with your finger tips.

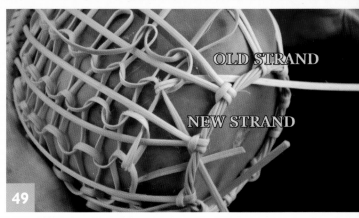

OLD STRAND

NEW STRAND

49

Plan to add a new knitting strand at the bottom of th column. Run the end of the completed strand under th lower ring. Begin the new strand under the lower ring an continue knitting.

50

Continue adding 6 loops in each column.

51

Use the Fid or awl to help insert the loops.

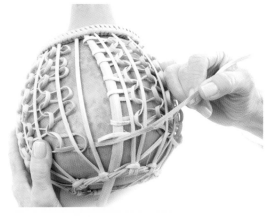

52

The final column has the wide tension reed in the way.

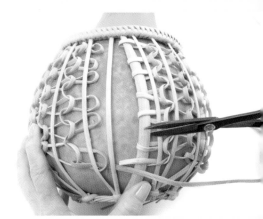

53

Remove the tension reed by cutting it in the middle.

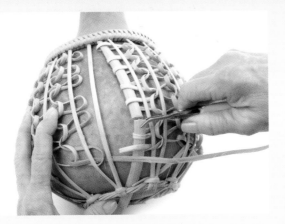

4 emove the lower section of the tension reed.

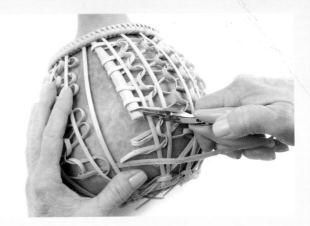

55 Carefully slide the upper section of the tension reed out of the first loops.

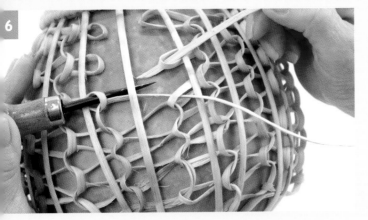

6 he first and last columns of knitting loops are laced together ith the remaining tail of flat oval from the previous column.

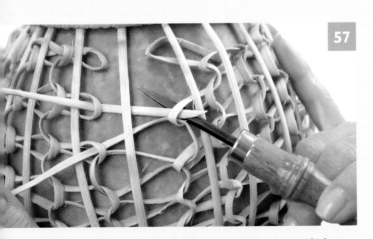

57 se the fid or awl to help guide the lacing strand, being reful to keep the loops consistent.

58 The knitting is finished and now it's time to weave the foot and the handle.

59

Make a ring from the 1-1/4" wide splint or bark.

60

We're using 1-1/4" wide ash splint in this example. T[.]
Ring has two layers. The long end will be cut flush with t[.]
starting end so that the thickness is uniform.

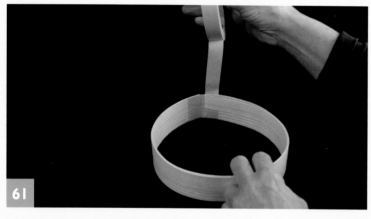

61

Use masking tape to secure the inner and outer ends of the splint to the ring.

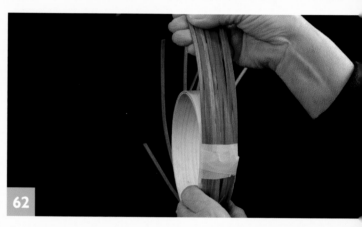

62

Cut 8 strands of the red dyed 1/4" flat reed 6" longer th[.]
the circumference of the ring. Line the 8 strands up a[.]
secure them to the ring with masking tape.

63

Begin weaving the base with a length of 1/4" undyed flat reed by passing it, from left to right, under 3 of the short red strands, then over 3 strands and finally, under the last 2 red strands.

64

Bring the natural strand around behind the ring and arou[.]
to the left. Weave over 1 red strand, under 3 red strand[.]
over 3 red strands and under the last red strand.

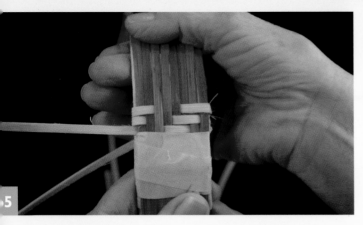

Wrap around the inside of the ring and weave over 2 red strands, under 3 and over 3 red strands.

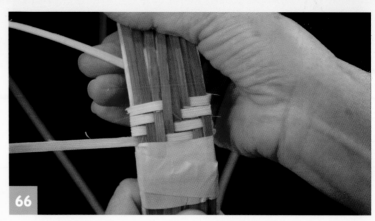

Wrap around the inside of the ring and weave over 3 red strands, under 3 and over 2 red strands.

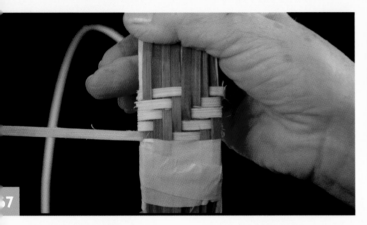

The fifth row is woven under 1 strand, over 3, under 3 and over 1 strand.

The 6th row is woven under 2 strands, over 3 strands, and under 3 strands.

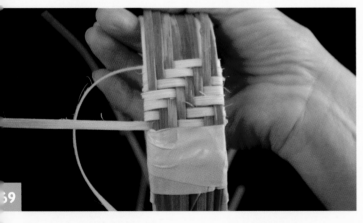

The 7th row begins the sequence again and replicates the first row by weaving under 3 strands, over 3 strands, and under 2 strands.

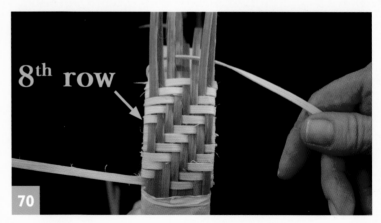

The 8th row is woven over 1 strand, under 3 strands, over 3 strands, and under 1 strand.

When you reach the end of a weaving strand, cut the end (**A**) flush with the right edge of the ring. Lay the new weaving strand (**B**) on top of the last weaving row (**A**).

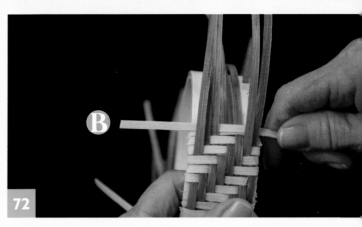

Pack the doubled weaving row against the last weaving ro[w] so that the pattern continues smoothly. The tail end (**B**) w[ill] be trimmed later.

To close up the weave, remove the tape that was holdin[g] the red strands originally. Trim both ends of the red strand[s] so that each row overlaps an inch.

The weaving continues as before. The tail end (**B**) will be trimmed flush with the left side of the ring.

If the pattern doesn't end exactly in the right place, it's oka[y]. Try to blend the weave so that the error isn't too obviou[s].

76

[C]ut one of the weaving strands into two thinner strips for [s]ecuring the base to the bottom of the gourd.

77

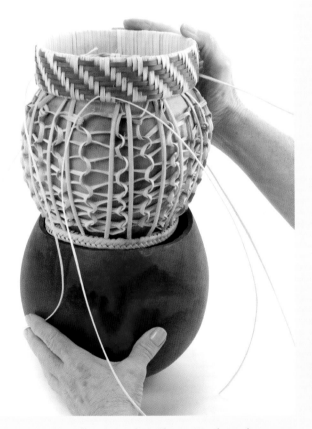

[In]vert the project gourd into a bowl or similar object to [k]eep the bottom upright. Secure the foot to the gourd in 3 [p]laces by lashing through the weave and around the vertical [la]shings on the bottom of the gourd.

78

Detail of the foot attachment.

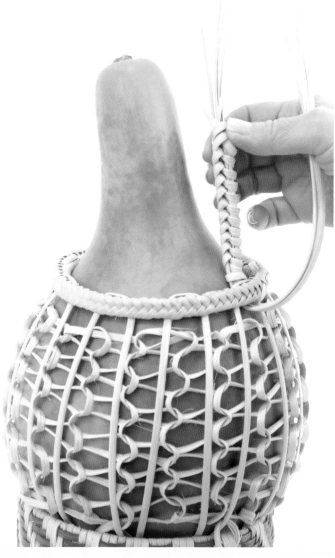

The handle is woven in the same way as the top ring at the beginning of the project except that the two ends of the ring are not joined before the weaving begins. Weave a third to one half of the handle, slide the unwoven section between the top ring and the gourd, then finishing the weaving and the joining of the two ends together.

Lash the top of the handle around the neck of the gourd t
secure it and trim the end.

The finished bottle.

GALLERY

TOP LEFT: Palm wine gourd from Senegal.
From the author's collection.
MIDDLE RIGHT: Ethiopian milk bottle wrapped with leather and
stitched with cowry shells.
From the collection of Ginger Summit.
BOTTOM LEFT: Black polypropylene netted hanger for gourd bottle.
From the author's collection.

An example of a Palm wine bottle from Cameroon.
From a private collection.

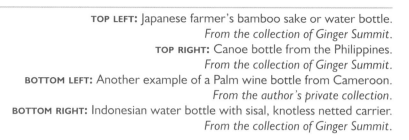

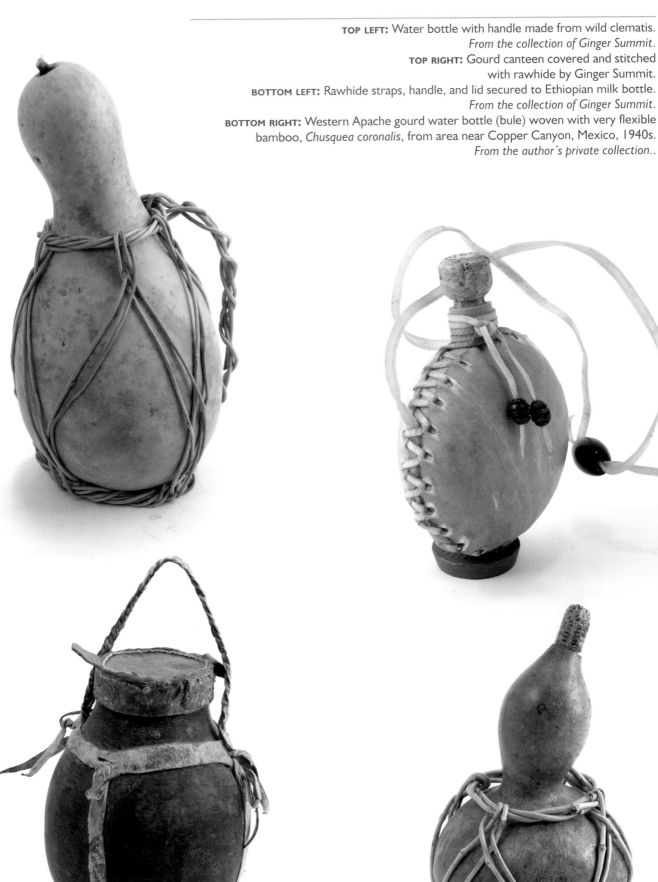

TOP LEFT: Water bottle with handle made from wild clematis. *From the collection of Ginger Summit.*
TOP RIGHT: Gourd canteen covered and stitched with rawhide by Ginger Summit.
BOTTOM LEFT: Rawhide straps, handle, and lid secured to Ethiopian milk bottle. *From the collection of Ginger Summit.*
BOTTOM RIGHT: Western Apache gourd water bottle (bule) woven with very flexible bamboo, *Chusquea coronalis*, from area near Copper Canyon, Mexico, 1940s. *From the author's private collection..*

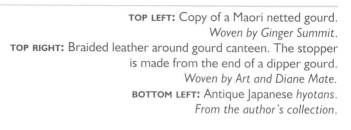

TOP LEFT: Copy of a Maori netted gourd.
Woven by Ginger Summit.
TOP RIGHT: Braided leather around gourd canteen. The stopper
is made from the end of a dipper gourd.
Woven by Art and Diane Mate.
BOTTOM LEFT: Antique Japanese *hyotans.*
From the author's collection.

TOP LEFT: Two gourd cups with 2.5mm rattan reel (chair cane) using technique from Cameroon palm wine gourd.
Woven by Marjorie Albright.
MIDDLE LEFT: Southeast Asian bamboo woven gourd bottle.
From the author's private collection.
BOTTOM LEFT: 1/2" flat oval reed covered gourd.
From the artist's private collection.
BOTTOM RIGHT: Woven and braided rattan ring and strap for hanging gourd bottle.
From the author's private collection.

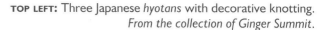
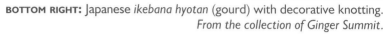
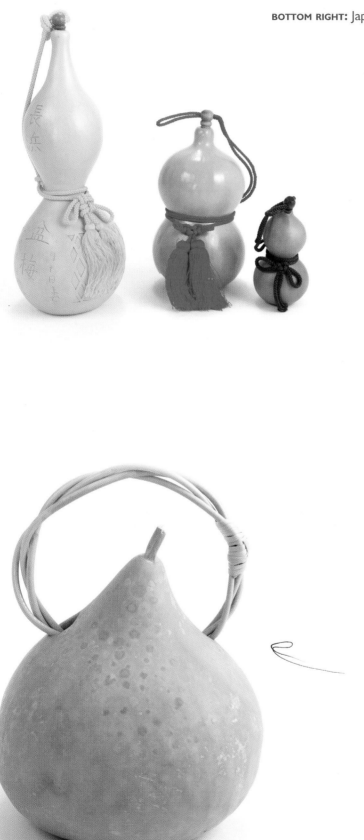

Koko with ʻumeke — Hawaiian carrying net with calabash.
Courtesy of David Young, artist and photographer.